ALCOHOLICS ARE LIARS

A Field Manual for High-Functioning
(Over)Drinkers

Tim Murphy

Alcoholics Are Liars: A Field Manual for High-Functioning (Over)Drinkers

By: Tim Murphy

ISBN for Print: 979-8-9934011-0-2

For permissions, contact: tim@7secretpillarsofsobriety.com

Cover & interior design: Rhianon Paige

Published by: AFGO Press

Printed in the United States

First Edition 2025

NOTICE: The information provided in this book is not to be construed as a substitute for medical advice or professional services of any kind. It is for educational purposes only. Neither the author nor the publisher make any representations or warranties, express or implied, about the accuracy, completeness, reliability, suitability, or availability with respect to the information, products, services, or related materials contained in this book for any purpose. The advice and strategies contained herein may not be suitable for your particular situation. Any use of this information is at your own risk.

In order to maintain confidentiality and ensure privacy, the author has used aliases, changed identifying details, and created composite stories based on a variety of clients with whom he has interacted.

To my daughter, Kimberly, and my sons, Ellis and Kyle. Thank you for your unconditional love, the kind that kept me going even when I didn't deserve it. You are my greatest reason and my greatest reward.

And to everyone out there who is ready to change their life. This book is for you. May it give you the courage to rise, the strength to stand, and the hope to believe that freedom is possible.

TABLE OF CONTENTS

BEFORE WE BEGIN...

Dear Reader,

Before we get started, thank you for picking up this book. I wrote it because I know exactly what it feels like to want more from life—and at the same time feel trapped by alcohol. It's a brutal tug-of-war. Part of you wants to do the right thing; part of you just wants relief. I've lived that fight.

To be clear, I'm not here to call you a liar. When I say alcoholics are liars, I don't mean it as an accusation. I mean it as a reminder: the first lie we tell is to ourselves, and it's the hardest one to let go of. I realize you're not trying to deceive anyone; it's just that the full weight of the truth can feel unbearable.

What I'm here to tell you is this: You're not broken. You don't need anyone's permission to change your life, except your own. **The Battle Ready Framework** I'll be sharing with you came out of my own experience as an alcoholic. It isn't a theory. It's survival. And it's proof that you can take back control *without* losing who you are.

If you'd like a quick way to get started, I invite you to take my **No Regret Quiz** on my website. It only takes a few minutes, but it'll show you truths you might have been avoiding, and it just might be the spark you need. Here's to permitting yourself to live free. Alcohol doesn't get the last word; you do.

With respect,

Tim Murphy

tim@7secretpillarsofsobriety.com

www.7secretpillarsofsobriety.com

From Addiction to Empowered Living

INTRODUCTION

Escaping High-Functioning Hell

I'm from a family that struggled with addiction. Both my parents were alcoholics.

And by extension, liars. They'd lie about being alcoholics. They'd lie about their drinking. They'd lie about lying.

It's what alcoholics do. I was no different. Denial is a powerful survival mechanism.

My father was a mean drunk. Abusive, both physically and verbally. He'd get drunk, shoot guns in the house, and threaten to kill us. Back me into a corner and tell me he was going to cut my ears off, *while* wielding a knife.

When I was a kid, I'd play "Connect the Dots" with the bullet holes in the wall. You know you've had an adventurous childhood when your favorite game growing up was Connect the Dots *with bullet holes in the walls!* Let's just say I got pretty good at drawing abstract art.

One night after bar hopping, I was on my way home when I blacked out, just as I'd done plenty of times before. I drove the car into the median and hit the divided highway sign so perfectly straight that it fell precisely down the middle of the car.

I didn't just hit it, I split it in half. It looked like I had done it on purpose; the sign crushed the top of the car down on me. I was a mile away from home and drove home looking through a shattered windshield.

You know the poem "The Road Not Taken" by Robert Frost? It's about a path that leads to a fork in the road, where you must decide to go one way or another. That divided highway sign was my fork in the road.

It felt like a message from the universe—with perfect aim.

One side said, "Keep going the way you've been going."

The other? "Turn around before all of this kills you."

⁂

I grew up swearing I'd never be like my father: abusive, angry, drunk, shooting holes in the walls.

And technically, I kept that promise in that I never fired a gun in the house. But that crash made me realize that I was still driving the rest of my life like a loaded weapon.

I was still on the path to becoming the very thing I swore I'd never be.

That night didn't kill me, but it cracked something open.

It forced me to stop pretending I had it under control.

That was the moment I stopped lying to myself. The night a road sign crushed my car became the night I decided to rebuild my life from the inside out. And that changed everything. That divided highway sign didn't just crush the roof of a car. It crushed the lies I'd been telling myself for years. And here's the kicker: It wasn't even my car. I'd borrowed it. After I wrecked it, I had to pay the owner for the damage. I drove it home looking through a shattered windshield, literally and figuratively.

I was a grown man playing Russian roulette with someone else's property… and my own life.

Because of alcohol.

That same week, my son had just been sentenced to 30 years in prison.

That wreck wasn't just a wake-up call. It was a warning shot. If I didn't change, I was either going to end up dead or in prison myself. And then, who would be left to support him? Who would show up for him? That moment forced me to stop pretending this was just "a bad night." It wasn't just about alcohol anymore. It was about responsibility. About legacy. About breaking the cycle I was born into—and refusing to pass it down one more generation. That's when everything shifted. Not because I hit "rock bottom." But because I finally looked at the wreckage—

literal and otherwise—and said: *No more.*

Like me, high-functioning alcoholics typically have more to lose and more motivation to change compared to those who have already lost important relationships, their jobs or careers, and may be incarcerated, homeless, or destitute.

Joining the military had been a pivotal turning point for me. It allowed me to be judged on my own merits rather than my family background or my last name. The military provided me with discipline, purpose, and a sense of identity that helped me avoid the same fate as my father. However, I still had the propensity for alcoholism, and living as one in that environment simply made me a very *different kind* of alcoholic.

At this point, I believe I can be considered "cured" of alcoholism. In fact, I no longer identify as an alcoholic, preferring the term "retired alcoholic." I now help other high-functioning alcoholics "retire" as my life's work. This book was born from my desire to prepare others to recover outside of the mainstream 12-step and similar programming and its emphasis on powerlessness and the lifelong "alcoholic" identity.

Mainstream recovery tells the alcoholic to surrender their lack of power over their drinking to a higher power outside of themselves. I tell the high-functioning alcoholic to reclaim the power they surrendered to the drinking. It's as simple as this: *If you do not take full responsibility for your drinking (and your life), you will remain in the cycle of high-functioning hell.*

I created a framework to help other high-functioning alcoholics save themselves with support. I ask that they take a stand to address the problem within, never surrender. This wasn't created based on a journal article or a basement conference in the 1930s. Battle Ready was forged from the battlefield of my own life. From the bitter truth that I could master chaos in uniform, but I couldn't manage ripples in my own glass. I didn't sit in a room and think up this structure with a whiteboard and a book of theory. I emerged from the wreckage—not just from the car crash that awful night—but from a life full of forgotten mornings, a failed marriage, and a career nearly lost.

This is why Battle Ready works when other programs do not. In particular, the ones that start with shame. They want you to declare yourself powerless, broken, defective. They leave you stuck in a one-size-fits-all box that was designed nearly a century ago for a world that no longer exists. Guys with security clearances, guys wearing the uniform, women leading national security teams—they don't miss the mark. The emphasis on shame and surrender backfires. It makes you drink in silence, in terror of being found out, as you pray no one realizes you're unraveling.

Battle Ready cuts through that. It's strategic. It's private. It's empowering. It hands you tools, not slogans. It confronts reality, not fairy tales. And it does so without taking away your dignity.

And believe me when I say, I understand how important your dignity is to you, even if you can't put it into words.

Becoming Battle Ready is your new mission briefing. This process works.

It builds strength so you can take a stand in your life against alcohol, and also against all the things that brought the alcohol into your life. Most importantly, I teach you how to take a stand for yourself and the things that are important to you. The things you regret missing out on. That's what this is all about.

The Battle Ready Framework works because it does not rely on fear; it's based on truth and strategic vision. It's not asking you to burn your life down to start over. It provides a system with which you can rebuild, even as you stand in the fire.

This isn't theory. This isn't group therapy. This is a battle-hardened protocol for men and women who are willing to do whatever it takes to stop drinking without annihilating their lives: their career, their happiness, their abilities, their relationships.

It works because it doesn't allow you to hide. It forces you to take a stand to recover.

You are not broken. You're not weak. You aren't some kind of screwed up human who can't "just handle it." It's just that no one ever gave you the tactics, techniques, and procedures. It is commonly accepted that alcohol consumption is a typical part of various occasions, often associated with celebration, coping mechanisms, and daily life. Nobody takes you aside and says, "Here's the alternative."

You hide it. You white-knuckle it. You silently continue to drink, wondering what in hell's name is standing in the way of you winning this battle.

Here is the absolute truth that no one else will tell you: *You have not failed. The system failed you.* The old recovery model was a one-size-fits-all model that didn't work for you. You say nothing because that's who you are, the military professional who has it in control. You don't see this stuff because of your relentless focus on a culture that upholds *freedom*. But here's the good news: Blindness is not forever. When the blind spot is uncovered, you can finally see what has been blocking you. You see it? You can't unsee it. That's where real change begins.

I'm not here to preach. I'm here to deliver the intel you lack. To show you there's a way out that doesn't involve shame, submission, or losing yourself. It's not like you need to be rebuilt from the ground up. You need to fight this battle on better terms. And what you have in your hands is just that.

Here's another truth: *If nothing changes, life does not explode overnight. It erodes over time.*

You will still wake up, still go to work, still shake people's hands and smile at the precisely correct moments. But beneath the surface, the slow seepage persists. The missed moments add up, baseball games you can't remember seeing, exchanges with your spouse that never penetrate beneath the surface, nights when your kids sought you out but discovered, instead, a glazed stare.

The price is not merely health, it's presence. It is that instead of here, really here, you are often somewhere else, somewhere in the fog. The brutal reality is you don't get those moments back.

Over time, the circle shrinks. Friends stop inviting you. Your family learns not to expect much. You begin to live smaller, convincing yourself it's "what has to be." The scary part? It is all normal, until you realize that's what you've built a life around: routine, regret, routine, regret, routine, regret.

Because the down-the-road effects are not just liver tests or DUIs. You wake up at one point, and you're *not* who you were supposed to be. You swapped possibility for ease, sex for self-sedation, and intimacy for a high that could never last. That's the real cost. Not flames, not madness, just a slow, noiseless death of everything inside you that asked for more.

Here is what I can say for sure: It's worth changing. The very second I stopped bargaining with alcohol and regained my power, things began to move. Not immediately, not magically, not unless the message is coming from somewhere with a lot of resources and power behind it, like the White House.

Hope roared into life the first morning I awoke clear-headed without that shame. Relationships began to mend, not because I apologized or sought forgiveness, but because I showed up differently. I was present. I was consistent. I was the guy people could trust again and, more importantly, the guy I could trust again.

The fog lifted. Work got sharper. My health began to rebuild. My family began leaning in rather than pulling back. For the first time in years, I didn't feel like I was barely hanging on; I felt alive, engaged, and even proud.

That is what is on the other side of this choice. Not a half-life spent whiffing and white-knuckling your way through twig-thin, but a full one spent waking up refreshed, lighthearted laughter without the flat note of regret, standing tall because you know you wrested control back.

The good news? You don't have to wipe out like I did. There's a firm, strategic groundwork to help you make your way through it. It's the one I used to rebuild my life, and in the next section, I'll lead you through it, step by step.

BECOMING BATTLE READY

Mike was a sharp, respected Master Sergeant, the kind of flight chief who held the shop together when everything else was coming apart. To his airmen and peers, he was steady, reliable, the guy who always had the answer.

On the surface, he looked unshakable.

But underneath, alcohol started running the show.

Alcohol had become his way of "decompressing" from deployments, from the stress of keeping his people alive, from the grind that never seemed to let up. His marriage was hanging by a thread. His kids were growing up without really knowing him.

What his colleagues didn't see was that the first drink of his day sometimes came before morning roll call. What started as a nightcap to take the edge off had turned into blacking out most nights. Mike called it his "moment of reckoning," the point where he realized he wasn't leading anyone, not even himself.

Sound familiar?

Mike's problem wasn't a lack of willpower or motivation. His problem was that every approach he'd tried was designed for *a different kind of alcoholic*: The homeless guy who's lost everything. The stereotypical "rock bottom" alcoholic who needs to surrender his will to a higher power because his own decision-making has led to unmitigated disaster.

But Mike hadn't lost everything. On the outside, anyway. He was still successful, still respected, still functional. He had too much to lose to risk the public shame of traditional recovery programs, and also too much to lose by continuing his current path. He needed an approach designed specifically for someone like him: someone who needed to solve this problem privately, strategically, and permanently.

That's exactly what my 4-step Battle Ready framework does.

Here's my line in the sand: *Unless you are willing to take full responsibility for your alcoholism, as opposed to turning it over to a "higher power" to guide you, you will struggle with true ownership of your recovery and therefore your life.* If you keep outsourcing your power, you will never be "cured" of the invisible chains that kept you drinking in the first place. Sobriety that leaves you powerless is just another form of control dressed up as surrender.

Most approaches to alcoholism recovery are built on outdated assumptions: that alcoholics are fundamentally different from other people, that addiction is a progressive disease that can only be managed (never cured), and that recovery requires surrendering your will to external forces, whether that's a twelve-step program, a higher power, or a treatment facility.

These approaches might work for people who have lost everything and have no other options. But if you're a high-functioning alcoholic who's still succeeding professionally while privately struggling, these methods aren't just ineffective. They're counterproductive. They're trying to break you down, when what you actually need is to build yourself back up.

A Different Path to Freedom

That's why I created the Battle Ready Framework: a strategic, private, empowering approach to alcoholism recovery designed specifically for high-functioning professionals who need real solutions, not shame-based programs that ask you to question the one-size-fits-all recovery model while keeping you drinking in silence.

In order that you can stand strong, you must first RISE, completing the following four steps in order:

Step 1: Real Awareness: Not the kind of awareness that comes from hitting rock bottom, but the kind that comes from applying analytical intelligence to your actual patterns, triggers, and costs. If you aren't willing to look beyond the alcohol, you're going to stay in high-functioning hell.

Step 2: Intentional Acceptance: Not accepting that you're powerless, but accepting the current reality of your situation so you can make strategic decisions about changing it. This isn't surrender: it's intelligence gathering that allows you to stop fighting the wrong battle.

Step 3: Strategic Accountability: Taking complete ownership of both the problem and the solution. If you don't take 100% responsibility for your sobriety, you will stay stuck in the cycle of high-functioning hell.

Step 4: Empowered Action: Action that flows from clarity and commitment, not desperation and shame. Building a recovery plan that actually works for you, not what you think you should follow.

This framework is designed for people who understand that alcoholics undergo a military-like training to become alcoholics—not intentionally, but systematically. Over time, the behaviors become disciplined, the routines ritualized, and the coping mechanisms get sharper, more efficient, more secretive.

There's a code of silence, a loyalty to the pattern, and a fierce resistance to surrender—much like the training of a soldier.

You built tolerance like endurance. You prepared for stress by numbing instead of strengthening. You adapted to function under pressure, often performing at a high level on the outside while quietly unraveling on the inside. It's a kind of training that doesn't start with one drink. It starts with a belief that "I'm not good enough," that asking for help is weakness, that holding it all together is the mission, and that vulnerability is dangerous.

Until you unlearn this training, you can't step into recovery. Until you rewrite the mission, you can't lead yourself out of the battle.

Specifically, the Battle Ready Framework works best for:

- High-functioning alcoholics who are still succeeding professionally but struggling privately; professionals in sensitive or high-responsibility roles who look for support outside the traditional recovery system because of stigma, job risk, or time constraints

- People who have more to lose and more motivation to change than their homeless, destitute, or otherwise noticeably impaired counterparts

- Those who understand that recovery becomes more sustainable when people feel empowered, safe, and respected rather than exposed, labeled, or shamed.

- Individuals ready to challenge the belief that sobriety means giving something up, when it's actually about reclaiming the inner authority you gave away long before the first drink

This approach is NOT for people who aren't "battle ready," and by that I mean, people who aren't mentally and emotionally prepared to face hard truths, commit to lasting change, and follow through on the transformation they *say* they want. Not because they're weak, but because they're still hoping for an easier way that doesn't require examining their relationship with discomfort, control, and vulnerability.

The biggest mindset shift required is understanding this: *Sobriety isn't just about removing the alcohol. It's about reclaiming the inner authority you gave away long before the first drink.* You have to be willing to examine the invisible chains that kept you drinking in the first place: the belief that you're not good enough without pharmaceutical assistance, that asking for help equals weakness, that you should be able to handle everything alone.

You have to be willing to question thought loops like "I deserve a drink" or "This is just how I unwind" and understand that these can be challenged and changed. You have to recognize that the same mental strength you use to succeed in your career can be applied to sobriety, if you're willing to direct it correctly instead of using it to maintain sophisticated self-deception.

Here's why the steps must be done in order:

Without **Real Awareness**, you're solving the wrong problem. You might think the problem is stress, a demanding job, bad luck, or a rough patch, believing alcohol is just a coping mechanism rather than understanding that your success is actually masking your dysfunction, not proving you're okay.

Without **Intentional Acceptance**, you're still making your recovery conditional on external circumstances changing first. You're still believing that if you haven't hit rock bottom, it's not that bad, or that you should be able to figure this out on your own.

Without **Strategic Accountability**, you're still waiting for someone else to save you, stuck between external blame and internal shame in a loop that keeps you from real action.

And without all three foundations in place, any action you take will be reactive rather than strategic, desperate rather than empowered, unsustainable rather than lasting. But the fourth step is **Empowered Action**, and by the time you have done the deep work of the first three steps, it will feel different than any other action you may have taken in the past. Easier. Natural.

Mike completed the Battle Ready Framework six months ago. He doesn't go to meetings, doesn't identify as an alcoholic, and doesn't rely on sponsors or higher powers to maintain his sobriety. *He simply doesn't want to drink anymore.* Not because he's afraid of the consequences, but because alcohol has become irrelevant to his life.

"I kept waiting for recovery to feel hard," he told me recently. "I kept waiting for cravings, for social pressure, for moments when I'd have to white-knuckle through temptation. But once I did the real work—understanding why I was drinking, accepting what needed to change, taking complete ownership of the solution—the action part felt natural. I wasn't fighting against alcohol anymore. I was building toward something better."

That's what the Battle Ready Framework creates: not a lifetime of fighting against your addiction, but a strategic process for eliminating your need for it entirely. You can rewire your habits, beliefs, and emotional triggers without shame-based programs.

Peace isn't earned through endless meetings. It's reclaimed through doing the inner work that only you can do. Are you ready to stop managing your alcoholism and start solving it? Are you ready to prove to yourself that you can cure yourself of alcoholism without wearing the labels people assign to you?

If so, then let's start with the foundation: developing the kind of Real Awareness that makes everything else possible.

STEP ONE

Real Awareness

The First Step Out of High-Functioning Hell

The military saved me.

I was already an alcoholic before I wore the uniform. When I joined the military, the culture of drinking alcohol made me feel at home. In the military, access was everywhere. There wasn't much need to hit bars off base when you had the Airmen's Club and the NCO Club right there. We played cards in the dorms, we drank, or we hit one of the clubs on base.

The culture of drinking didn't corrupt me; it welcomed me. I wasn't "becoming" an alcoholic—I was already at home in it. What the military did was give me cover. As long as I performed, nobody questioned how deep I was in. I could lead, achieve, and earn respect during the day; nobody asked how many nights ended with me passed out.

The drinks before work started as "liquid courage," just a quick shot to calm the nerves before a particularly stressful assignment. Then it became routine maintenance, like checking your gear or polishing your boots. Essential preparation for the day ahead. I told myself it was management, not dependency. Control, not chaos. I was functioning at the highest level, so how could there be a problem?

That's the insidious nature of high-functioning alcoholism; it hides in plain sight, disguised as competence and wrapped in success.

You're probably sitting where I was then, wondering if you're making too big a deal out of this. Maybe you're thinking, "I'm not like those people in the movies—I don't drink in the morning, I don't miss work, I don't get arrested." You're right. You're not like them. You're something else entirely, and in many ways, that makes your situation more dangerous, not less.

Here's what I wish someone had told me back then: Your success isn't proof that you're okay, it's proof that you're exceptionally good at managing a problem that's slowly eating you alive from the inside.

Let me be clear about something that flies in the face of conventional recovery wisdom: You are not powerless. You didn't lose control because you're fundamentally broken or diseased. You lost awareness, and that's something you can absolutely reclaim. The same mental discipline that makes you successful in your career, the same strategic thinking that got you where you are, the same problem-solving skills you use every day… all of that is still there. You just need to turn those tools inward.

But first, you need to see what's really happening.

I work with executives, healthcare professionals, lawyers, and military officers. In other words, my clients are people who have everything to lose and who've gotten very good at managing their public image while their private reality slowly unravels. They come to me because they've reached a point where the mental gymnastics required to maintain the illusion of control are exhausting them more than the alcohol itself.

Like you, they've undergone a military-like training to become functional alcoholics. Not intentionally, but over time, the behaviors became disciplined, the routines ritualized, the coping mechanisms sharper and more efficient. They built tolerance like endurance, prepared for stress by numbing instead of strengthening, and learned to function under pressure while quietly unraveling inside.

⁂

Dennis was the best worker in the office, the guy everyone counted on, the one who could juggle a heavy workload and still outperform the rest of the team. On paper, he was untouchable. He was respected and set the standard. But beneath that polished exterior, alcohol was starting to creep into his professionalism.

His so-called "wake-up call" wasn't a DUI or a pink slip; it was catching himself structuring his entire day around when he could take that first drink. Breath mints became a permanent fixture in his pocket. He checked his watch constantly during late-afternoon meetings, not out of boredom but out of irritation that they were cutting into happy hour. And if the boss asked him to stay late? The discomfort wasn't about the workload; it was because it meant delaying the only part of the day when he thought he could relax.

"I'm not an alcoholic," he told me during our first talk. "I just drink too much because my job is stressful."

Sound familiar?

Here's the thing about awareness: It requires you to stop managing the narrative and start examining the facts. Not the story you tell yourself about why you drink, but the actual patterns. Not your intentions about moderating, but your actual behavior. Not what you're able to accomplish despite your drinking, but what you're unable to access because of it.

You probably believe the problem is stress, a demanding job, bad luck, or a rough patch. You think alcohol is just a coping mechanism, not the root of the problem. You may tell yourself, "I just need to get through this season," or "I drink too much, but it's not like I've hit rock bottom."

But you're starting to realize that your drinking is causing real harm—emotionally, physically, and relationally. You've lost control over something that once felt more controllable. What you don't yet understand is that you can rewire your habits, beliefs, and emotional triggers without shame-based programs. You underestimate your ability to build internal accountability without external punishment or labels.

The military taught me that situational awareness can be the difference between life and death. In recovery, awareness can be the difference between freedom and a lifetime of sophisticated self-deception.

This is why Real Awareness has to be the first step, not something you get around to eventually. Without it, you're operating on faulty intelligence. You're making strategic decisions based on incomplete or distorted information. You're solving the wrong problem.

Most traditional recovery programs skip right past Real Awareness and jump straight to surrender: admitting you're powerless, turning your will over to a higher power, accepting that you'll always be "in recovery." But how can you surrender something you don't fully understand? How can you fix what you haven't accurately diagnosed?

That approach might work for people who've lost everything and have nowhere else to turn. But you? You still have options. You still have leverage. You still have the capacity to think your way through this... *if* you're willing to look clearly at what's actually happening.

The Real Awareness I'm talking about isn't the kind that comes from hitting rock bottom or having an intervention. The sharp edge of awareness for my clients will come from applying the same analytical skills you use in your professional life to your relationship with alcohol. It's recognizing patterns, identifying triggers, and understanding the real cost-benefit analysis of your current approach.

When I work with clients who possess this level of calculated awareness, they often tell me it's simultaneously relieving and terrifying. Relieving, because they finally have accurate information to work with. Terrifying, because that information makes it impossible to keep pretending everything is fine. It's right there, like data on a spreadsheet.

The cost of every drink is obvious.

Jeff, an IT Specialist, put it this way: "Once I saw how much mental bandwidth I was using to manage my drinking—planning it, hiding it, recovering from it, worrying about it—I realized I was operating at maybe 70% capacity, not just in Information Technology, not in terms of job performance or 'potential' but in everything. I was so focused on maintaining the illusion that I was 'fine' that I couldn't see how much *energy* that was costing me. And what I could have done with that energy, that's the part that I found unacceptable to continue."

That's what Real Awareness reveals: the hidden costs. Not just the obvious ones like hangovers or embarrassing moments, but the subtle erosion of your mental clarity, emotional availability, and genuine confidence. The energy you spend managing your image instead of improving your life. The relationships that suffer not because you're falling down drunk, but because you're emotionally unavailable or defensive about your choices. Or simply staying in to drink and watch TV instead of nurturing the goals and dreams you once had.

Real Awareness means acknowledging that you've been running a sophisticated operation designed to maintain the status quo while part of you slowly dies. It means recognizing that the very skills that make you successful—planning, compartmentalization, performance under pressure—have been co-opted to serve your drinking rather than your life goals.

Again, this isn't about shame or judgment. Military operations fail when intelligence is incomplete or compromised. Recovery fails for the same reason. You can't execute an effective strategy based on bad information or wishful thinking.

You're unaware that you're stuck in thought loops—like "I

deserve a drink" or "This is just how I unwind"—loops that can be challenged and changed. You don't realize that the same mental strength you use to succeed in your career can be applied to sobriety, if you're willing to direct it toward building solutions instead of maintaining sophisticated self-deception.

The clients I can't help are the ones who aren't ready for this level of honesty with themselves. Perhaps they want a solution that doesn't require them to examine their current approach too closely. Some may want to moderate without acknowledging why moderation hasn't worked so far. There are always plenty who expect to change their drinking without changing their thinking.

That's not cowardice. It's just not being battle-ready—not yet. And that's okay. But if you're reading this book, something tells me you're different. Something tells me you're tired of managing the problem and ready to solve it.

Here's what most people don't realize: The same mental strength you use to excel in high-pressure situations can be redirected toward sobriety. The same discipline that got you where you are professionally can be applied to rewiring your relationship with alcohol. The same strategic thinking that makes you valuable in your career can be used to design a recovery that actually works for your life.

However, none of that ever happens without first doing the deep work of Real Awareness.

You need to see clearly before you can act decisively. You need accurate intelligence before you can plan effective operations. You need to understand what you're actually dealing with before you can determine the best approach to handle it.

Without **Real Awareness,** *you'll keep cycling through the same patterns—periods of control followed by periods of excess, promises to yourself that you don't keep, sophisticated rationales for why this time is different.* With awareness, you can begin to see those patterns for what they are: learned behaviors that can be unlearned, thought loops that can be interrupted, and emotional triggers that can be addressed directly rather than numbed.

This is why Real Awareness is the first step, and it must not be skipped. It's not just the first step—it's the foundation everything else is built on. Without it, you're not recovering; you're just rearranging the furniture in the same house. You might change when you drink, or what you drink, or how much you drink, but you haven't changed the fundamental relationship between you and alcohol—or yourself. That relationship discovery is what determines whether any other changes will last.

※

Tracy came to me convinced he "just liked to unwind." His work record was spotless, his reputation solid, but inside, he knew he was running on fumes. Our first step wasn't taking away the bottle; it was taking inventory. I had him track everything: how many drinks, when, what triggered them, and what the aftermath looked like. Within two weeks, he saw what he'd avoided for years: alcohol wasn't relaxing him; it was stealing his mornings, numbing his presence with his kids, and creeping into his work. That's Real Awareness. Not rock-bottom drama, but honest intel. When Tracy saw the pattern in black and white, he couldn't unsee it. And that's when change became possible.

Real Awareness, done completely and with brutal honesty, is what separates temporary sobriety from permanent freedom. It's what allows you to move beyond white-knuckling through alcohol cravings to actually eliminating them. It's what transforms you from someone who *doesn't* drink to someone who doesn't *want* to drink, not even in a setting that might have felt impossible without alcohol before.

Of course, awareness alone isn't enough. Once you clearly understand what you're dealing with, you must be willing to accept what that information means about your current approach and your need for a different strategy. You have to be willing to acknowledge that the methods you've been using—willpower, moderation, managing the symptoms—aren't going to get you where you want to go. Remember, this is not the powerless kind of acceptance that traditional recovery promotes, but the strategic kind that allows you to stop fighting the wrong battle and start winning the right war.

Are you ready to see what you're actually dealing with? Are you prepared to trade comfortable illusions for uncomfortable truths? Because once you develop real awareness, there's no going back to pretending everything is fine. But there's also no moving forward without it.

The question here isn't whether you can handle the truth about your drinking. You deal with difficult truths all the time, difficult responsibilities, and difficult balancing acts. The question I have is whether you can afford to keep avoiding it.

STEP TWO

Intentional Acceptance

The Truth That Sets You Free

For years, I thought acceptance meant giving up. I thought it meant admitting defeat, waving the white flag, surrendering to something bigger than myself. The military doesn't exactly teach you that acceptance is a strength. It teaches you to overcome, adapt, and push through. Improvise, adapt, and overcome. So when I first heard about "accepting" my alcoholism, everything in me rebelled against it.

What I didn't understand then was that I was already accepting something—I was accepting a life of sophisticated misery. I was accepting that alcohol was my primary coping mechanism. I was accepting that I needed something outside myself to function. I was accepting that this was just how things were going to be. I just wasn't calling it "acceptance" because it felt more like "management."

The hardest part wasn't accepting that I drank too much. Hell,

I knew that. The hardest part was accepting what that really meant about how I'd been living.

I had to accept that my ability to perform under pressure—something I'd always prided myself on—wasn't actually a strength. It was conditioning. Survival mode dressed up as discipline. I had to accept that what I called "having a few drinks to unwind" was actually my central nervous system's desperate attempt to downshift from a state of constant hypervigilance that had become my normal.

Most of all, I had to accept that no one was coming to save me. There would be no intervention, no rock-bottom moment dramatic enough to force change, no external circumstances that would finally make quitting feel easy or inevitable. It was all on me.

If you're reading this, you probably know exactly what I'm talking about.

You've been waiting for that moment when quitting will feel necessary rather than optional. When the consequences will be severe enough to override your resistance. When someone else will care enough about your drinking to make it their problem too.

But I'm going to tell you the thing that no one wants to hear: that moment may never come. High-functioning alcoholics often never hit the kind of rock bottom that forces change.

Your competence protects you from consequences.

Your success insulates you from interventions.

Your ability to manage *the symptoms* keeps you from addressing the cause.

That's both your blessing and your curse.

I've worked with clients who've been waiting decades for their "moment of clarity" or their "wake-up call." Meanwhile, they're slowly eroding from the inside—emotionally, physically, spiritually—while maintaining a perfectly acceptable exterior. They're dying by degrees while everyone around them thinks they're fine.

Chris was the kind of employee every office wanted: sharp, dependable, the one who could carry the heavy load when others couldn't. For years, alcohol stayed hidden behind the mask of his performance. He still made it to work and did not miss a deadline. To anyone looking from the outside, Chris seemed to have it all together.

Then the system started showing cracks. He always had a breath mint in his mouth and took long bathroom breaks that weren't about the bathroom. There were daytime "disappearances" after lunch. He started calling in sick on Mondays a little too often. His once-sharp reports showed typos and missed details. Deadlines started slipping. Coworkers whispered about his forgetfulness, his sloppy work, and his distracted presence in meetings.

Chris thought he was still fooling everyone, but the truth was obvious: alcohol was writing itself into his daily routine. The minor lapses were becoming the norm. What was once excellence had become mediocrity, and everyone could see it.

When we talked, he admitted the truth: he felt like crap most mornings, and most nights ended in a blur. He planned his evenings around drinking and his mornings around recovering. The only reason he could function was due to his past reputation as a superstar in the office. But he realized his life was falling apart.

That's the reality of high-functioning drinking: You don't collapse all at once. You bleed out slowly.

The Intentional Acceptance I'm talking about isn't the powerless kind that traditional recovery programs promote. It's not about admitting you're broken or diseased or fundamentally different from other people. It's about accepting the current reality of your situation so you can make informed decisions about what to do next.

This step must follow awareness because you can't accept what you don't see clearly. But it has to come before you can take meaningful action because you can't solve a problem you're still minimizing or misunderstanding.

Intentional Acceptance means acknowledging that alcohol has become your solution—not just to stress or boredom or social anxiety, but to the fundamental discomfort of being you without pharmaceutical assistance. It means accepting that what started as a choice has become a dependency, even if that dependency looks different from what you imagined dependency would look like.

It means accepting that you've been blaming external circumstances for an internal condition. Your job stress doesn't make you drink—it reveals that you haven't developed effective ways to process stress without numbing. Your difficult relationships don't make you drink—they reveal that you haven't learned to navigate conflict or disappointment without escaping. Your past trauma doesn't make you drink—it reveals that you haven't processed those experiences in a way that allows you to move forward.

This isn't victim-blaming. It's reality-checking. And it's actually the most empowering realization you can have because it means you have more control than you thought.

᪥

Jennifer, a nurse practitioner, came to me after what she called her "moment of reckoning." She'd been working overtime during the pandemic, using alcohol to decompress after impossibly difficult shifts. "I kept telling myself I was drinking because of COVID, because of the stress, because of what I was seeing at work," she told me. "But then I realized I was drinking the same way before COVID. I was drinking the same way before I became a nurse. The circumstances kept changing, but my response stayed exactly the same."

That's Intentional Acceptance. Not accepting that you're powerless, but accepting that you've been using the same coping mechanism for different problems for years—and it's not working anymore.

You have to accept that you've been stuck between external blame and internal shame, and that loop keeps you from real action. You blame past trauma or family dysfunction, toxic relationships, work pressure, the systems, or recovery programs that don't meet your needs. But deep down, you shame yourself and feel like you should be stronger, have more willpower.

You wonder why you can crush it at work but can't quit drinking.

Intentional Acceptance admits that the very qualities that make you successful—your ability to compartmentalize, to perform under pressure, to push through discomfort—have been hijacked by your relationship with alcohol. Your discipline has become a tool for managing your drinking rather than directing your life. Your problem-solving skills have become focused on maintaining your habit rather than pursuing your goals.

You have to accept that needing help isn't a weakness, it's *wisdom*. You can't think your way out of a problem you thought your way into unless you change your thinking. The strategies and tactics that got you this far into your life with alcohol in control aren't going to get you where you want to go.

Sobriety isn't about losing something... it's about gaining everything back. Your mental clarity, your emotional availability, your genuine confidence, your authentic relationships, your actual dreams rather than the numbed-down versions you've been settling for.

But here's where my approach differs radically from traditional recovery: I don't ask you to accept that you're powerless. I ask you to accept that you're powerful enough to change this. It is purely a matter of applying your power in the right direction.

That's how Battle Ready works in real life. Not abstract principles, but real people taking back control, step by step, phase by phase. Awareness, Acceptance, Accountability, Action. Each one is a weapon in the fight, and together they form a strategy that works. Notice, I don't ask you to accept that you'll always be "in recovery." Recovery, in my program, is a process with a definitive endpoint. You can become someone who simply doesn't want to drink, and not remain someone who wants to drink but can't.

I don't ask you to accept that alcohol will "always" be a struggle. I ask that you accept the struggle exists now so that you can do the work to eliminate it permanently.

This level of Intentional Acceptance is terrifying for most people because it removes all the comfortable excuses. You can't blame your job, your family, your past, or your brain chemistry. You can't wait for external circumstances to improve or for motivation to strike or for someone else to care enough to intervene. *You do have to accept that this is your problem to solve, your life to reclaim, your potential to fulfill.*

৵

Maria had spent her entire career in the military mastering control. But alcohol was the one battle she couldn't win. Every program she tried told her to "surrender" and admit she was powerless.

That language made her shut down—she didn't surrender to *anything*. Instead, I coached her into Intentional Acceptance. There's no surrender, nor weakness. Just a clear-eyed acknowledgment of reality. She accepted that alcohol was running her life, that it was costing her relationships, and that it was eroding her health. She didn't wave the white flag; she gathered intel. She stopped fighting the wrong battles (shame, denial, blame) and redirected her energy toward a smarter fight.

Acceptance didn't mean defeat—it was tactical clarity.

But here's what happens when you truly and intentionally accept this: everything changes. Intentional Acceptance allows you to stop wasting energy on things you can't control and redirect that energy toward things you can.

When you accept that alcohol has become your primary coping mechanism, you can start developing better ones. When you accept that you've been avoiding difficult emotions, you can start learning to process them. When you accept that you've been living in survival mode, you can start building a life worth being fully present for. When you accept that no one else is responsible for your sobriety, you can stop waiting for external validation or perfect circumstances and start creating internal motivation and better conditions.

This is why Intentional Acceptance can't be skipped. Without it, you'll keep trying to solve the wrong problem. You'll keep looking for ways to manage your drinking instead of ways to eliminate your need for it. You'll keep treating symptoms instead of causes. You'll keep giving your power away to circumstances, other people, or programs that don't understand your specific situation.

With Intentional Acceptance, you can finally start building a recovery that actually works for your life instead of against it. You can start using your strengths—your intelligence, your discipline, your problem-solving abilities—to design a sustainable approach to sobriety instead of using those same strengths to maintain an unsustainable relationship with alcohol.

Acceptance isn't the end of the process—it's the beginning of real change. It's what allows you to move from managing the problem to solving it. From surviving your life to designing it. From being a victim of your circumstances to being the architect of your future.

But acceptance without action is just sophisticated resignation. Once you accept the reality of your situation and your responsibility for changing it, you have to be willing to take complete ownership of the solution. You have to be willing to stop making excuses and start making different choices.

Are you ready to accept not just your problem, but your power to change it? Because everything that happens next depends on your answer to that question.

STEP THREE

Strategic Accountability

The End of the Blame Game

Jason is not just an alcoholic. He's a man who's been trained, intentionally or not, to rely on alcohol like it's standard issue gear in a long, silent war. He's been conditioned to stay composed under fire, even when he's burning inside, numb instead of talking. His code was simple: Function under pressure, not feel through it, and treat vulnerability like an enemy combatant.

This isn't just a drinking problem. It's a whole survival-mode protocol gone rogue. He's slipping at work, worrying about the next misstep. He fears losing control in public or at family events. He doesn't feel at peace. He feels like he's still deployed, even at home. What he hasn't been told is that he can retrain his mind the same way he once trained his body and behavior. But this time, the mission isn't to survive. It's *to come home whole*. The catch? No one is going to send him to training or sign orders for this mission except *himself*.

I always knew I had a drinking problem. Deep down, past all the rationalizations and mental gymnastics, I *knew*. But knowing and accepting are two different things, sometimes very different, and accepting something and taking accountability for it can be in completely different universes.

For years, I lived in the space between knowing and doing something about it. I told myself I could quit anytime I wanted, but I just didn't want to quit yet. I had good reasons: the stress of military life, the culture of drinking that surrounded me, and the fact that I was still performing at a high level. I had a thousand explanations for why now wasn't the right time, why my situation was different, why I deserved this one vice.

What I didn't have was accountability. And without accountability, knowledge is just information, and acceptance is just acknowledgment. Neither one creates change.

The absence of accountability in my life looked like a masterclass in sophisticated avoidance. I would go through periods where I'd cut back, moderate, or even abstain for days or weeks. I'd feel proud of my self-control, convinced that this proved I wasn't really addicted. Then something stressful would happen—a difficult mission, relationship conflict, disappointment of some kind—and I'd be right back to my old patterns.

Each time this cycle repeated, I'd blame external circumstances. If my commanding officer wasn't such a hardass, if my family understood the pressure I was under, if the military culture wasn't so toxic, if I had better coping mechanisms... always something outside my control that made drinking feel *necessary*.

The cost of this blame game was enormous, though I couldn't

see it at the time. Every external excuse I made was energy I wasn't putting toward actual solutions. Every time I pointed the finger at circumstances, I was essentially saying I had no power to change my situation. I was trading temporary comfort for long-term helplessness.

The most expensive drug you will ever buy is comfort. Pricier than whiskey, deadlier than beer. It seems innocuous... safety, predictability, routine, but it saps you, steadily, like a silent bleed you don't realize you're feeling, until you're cold.

When you remain safe, you miss out on the battlefield that makes you. You avert the fire that would have made you sharper, stronger, alive. There is a risk where the blood flows. Risk is where growth happens. Without it, you atrophy. You sit there and rot while telling yourself you're "fine."

What stays dormant? Your potential. The man you could have been, the present father, the loyal spouse, the leader who actually leads, remains locked away in the cage of "maybe someday." You never hone the blade because you never enter the fight.

What ends? Drive. Spirit. You need to be able to look in the mirror and know you're not bullshitting yourself. That's what dies. Each time you pick the easy pour over the hard decision, you go a little dark, not all at once. Just slow enough to make you think you're alive.

Avoidance of risk does not make you safe; it makes you dead while you are still breathing. You don't flame out; you fade into insignificance. That is the price of comfort in the end: You exchange the life you were made to live for the one where you're barely surviving.

If you're reading this, you've probably been living in that same space—caught between knowing you have a problem and taking full ownership of solving it. You know your drinking has gotten out of hand, but you've got reasons. Good reasons. Legitimate reasons that anyone in your situation would understand.

Your job is incredibly stressful. Your spouse doesn't appreciate what you do. Your boss is unreasonable. Your industry is toxic. Your family has a history of alcoholism, so you're fighting your genetics. The pandemic changed everything. Your teenagers are impossible. Your aging parents need more care than you can give. The political climate has everyone on edge.

All of these things might be true. Hell, most of them probably are true. But here's what I learned the hard way: you can be 100% right about your circumstances and 100% stuck in your situation at the same time.

The brutal truth is that nobody else is going to fix your drinking problem. Your boss isn't going to become less demanding. Your industry isn't going to become less toxic. Your family history isn't going to change. Your circumstances might improve temporarily, but there will always be new stressors, new disappointments, new reasons to drink.

Strategic Accountability isn't about blame; it's about power. When you blame external circumstances for your drinking, you're essentially admitting that you're powerless to change your situation until those circumstances change first. When you take accountability strategically, you're claiming your power to respond differently regardless of what's happening around you.

※

Mark was sharp, respected, and high-performing. But he was hiding in plain sight, showing up with mints in his pocket, skipping out early for happy hour, and dragging through Monday mornings. With coaching, we moved him into Strategic Accountability. I made it clear: if he wanted change, he had to own it 100%. No blaming stress, no pointing at culture, no waiting for someone else to save him. He built structures: daily check-ins, accountability with a trusted peer, and complicated rules about when and where alcohol could no longer show up. The shift was brutal at first, but also very freeing. When Mark stopped outsourcing responsibility and took back control, he started to come alive again. That's when he started winning the right battles.

This is exactly why you can't skip from acceptance to action. There's a crucial step in between where you stop making your sobriety conditional on other people's behavior or external circumstances improving. You stop waiting for motivation to strike or willpower to magically appear, and stop treating your recovery like something that happens to you.

It's crucial that you start treating it like something you actively create.

❧

Lisa, a marketing executive, came to me after her third attempt at moderation failed spectacularly. "I keep waiting for life to calm down so I can focus on my drinking," she told me. "But life never calms down. There's always something: a product launch, a difficult client, a family crisis. I'm starting to think I'm using stress as an excuse to avoid dealing with this."

That was her Strategic Accountability moment: recognizing that she'd been making her sobriety dependent on conditions that would never exist.

As a coach and a military man, I'm not one to let anyone off the hook. The mission comes first. Stay the course. Push through. When a client commits, I commit. This is not something you ever have to do alone.

Real personal accountability looks like acknowledging that you have a problem, even if you're "not like those other alcoholics." It looks like letting go of the belief that someone else needs to change first—your employer, your spouse, your parents, the recovery industry. *It looks like choosing a recovery path that fits your life instead of the one you think you should follow or the one that worked for someone else.*

Most importantly, it looks like owning your story instead of hiding from it. Not because you're to blame for everything that contributed to your drinking, but because you're the only one who can change what happens next.

The power of Strategic Accountability is that it transforms you from a victim of circumstances into an architect of solutions. Instead of waiting for external conditions to improve, you start creating internal conditions for success. Instead of reacting to what happens to you, you start responding from a place of choice and intention.

Instead of lying to yourself, you tell the truth.

This directly supports my core claim: *Unless you're willing to take full responsibility for your alcoholism, as opposed to turning it over to a "higher power" to guide you, you will struggle with true ownership of your recovery and therefore your life.* You'll also keep on lying to *yourself.*

If you keep outsourcing your power, you will never be "cured" of the invisible chains that kept you drinking in the first place.

Traditional recovery programs often skip real accountability and jump straight to surrender—admitting powerlessness and turning your will over to something else. But how can you turn over something you have never fully claimed? How can you surrender responsibility you haven't even taken?

My approach requires you to take complete ownership first.

Not because you caused all your problems, but because you're the only one who can solve them. Not because you're to blame for your past, but because you're responsible for your future.

When I work with clients, I often say, "If you think it, ink it." Write down what you're actually dealing with. Document your patterns, your triggers, your excuses, your attempts at change. Not to shame yourself, but to get clear on what you're taking responsibility for.

Most people are shocked when they see their own patterns laid out on paper. The cycle becomes obvious: drink, feel guilty, promise to change, get triggered, drink again. The external circumstances change, but the response stays the same. The same *stress-drink-regret-repeat* pattern plays out regardless of whether the trigger is work pressure, relationship conflict, boredom, celebration, or disappointment.

That's when Strategic Accountability becomes powerful; when you can see clearly that you've been responding to different situations with the same coping mechanism for years, when you realize that changing your circumstances hasn't changed your patterns, when you understand that your relationship with alcohol is about you, not about what's happening to you.

Strategic Accountability means doing the inner work no one else can do for you. Not because you're to blame for your conditioning—the military-like training that taught you "I'm not good enough," that asking for help is weakness, that holding it all together is the mission, and vulnerability is dangerous. You're not to blame for learning those patterns, *but you are responsible for unlearning them.*

Just like in combat, that mindset might have helped you survive the battle, but it will cost you peace in the aftermath. Until you unlearn the training, you can't step into recovery. Until you rewrite the mission, you can't lead yourself out of the battle.

Strategic Accountability has to come before any action will stick because, without it, your actions will be reactive rather than strategic. You'll be trying to manage symptoms instead of addressing causes. You'll be working around your problems instead of through them.

With Strategic Accountability, powered by the work of Real Awareness and Intentional Acceptance, you can start building a recovery plan based on what actually works for your brain, your schedule, your personality, and your goals rather than what you think you should do or what worked for someone else. You can start addressing the underlying patterns that drive your drinking instead of just trying to control the drinking itself.

But most importantly, accountability gives you permission to succeed. When you're still blaming external circumstances, part of you is always waiting for those circumstances to change first. You're holding back from full commitment because at least some part of you is still not sure it's wholly your responsibility to fix this. Once you take complete accountability, you can throw your full weight behind your recovery. You can invest in solutions instead of managing problems. You can build new systems instead of just trying to control old behaviors. You can start living like someone who doesn't drink instead of someone who's trying not to drink.

Strategic Accountability isn't a one-time decision; it's a daily choice to respond from a place of ownership instead of victimhood. To focus on what you can control instead of what you can't. To invest your energy in solutions instead of excuses.

The clients I can't help are the ones who want to get sober without taking full responsibility for their sobriety. They want me to give them tools and strategies while they continue to blame their drinking on external circumstances. They want to change their relationship with alcohol without changing their relationship to personal responsibility. That doesn't work, not because I'm unwilling to help, but because lasting change requires ownership. You can't build sustainable sobriety on the foundation of conditional commitment and external blame.

᠅

Jason told me he was "tired of surviving." He wasn't on the streets; he wasn't in legal trouble, but he was missing everything that mattered. His wife had learned not to expect much from him, and his kids were growing up without the version of their dad they deserved.

With coaching, we moved into Empowered Action. Not just talk, not theory, but steps. He replaced his after-work drinking ritual with a new one: walking his daughter to the park. He rebuilt his evenings around connection instead of isolation. He joined a group where he wasn't hiding but leading.

For the first time, he wasn't just sober, he was alive. Action gave him momentum, and momentum gave him pride. He depended on me less and less. He became mentally fit. He was running his own mission.

Once you take Strategic Accountability—once you own your patterns, your choices, and your power to change them— everything becomes possible. You're no longer waiting for permission from your circumstances to get better, and that means you're ready to create the conditions for recovery regardless of what's happening around you. Having made that shift, real action becomes not just possible, but inevitable.

STEP FOUR

Empowered Action

When Clarity Meets Momentum

When James first reached out to me, he didn't call himself an alcoholic. In his words, he was just "burned out."

It's just another way we lie to ourselves.

And to reiterate, I'm never accusing anyone of being an alcoholic or a liar. What I'm calling out are the half-truths we tell ourselves just to survive. They're not lies meant to deceive others; they're the lies we cling to because admitting the whole truth feels impossible to bear.

James had a respectable government job, a family that depended on him, and a reputation for being dependable. From the outside, he looked fine. Inside, he felt exhausted. He admitted that every evening was planned around alcohol, every morning was a battle to hide the fog, and every excuse he told himself started to sound hollow.

At first, James wasn't even sure he wanted help. He had tried other programs before and hated how powerless they made him feel. What drew him to my method was simple: I wasn't offering slogans. I wasn't telling him he was broken. I was offering him a strategic way to rebuild his life without stripping away who he was. That gave him enough courage to take the first step.

The first step was Real Awareness. James tracked his patterns the way he would track intel on a mission: when he drank, what triggered it, and what it cost him. It didn't take long before the truth slapped him in the face. Alcohol wasn't stress relief; it was *the source* of most of his stress. He saw the missed moments with his kids, the half-hearted conversations with his wife, and the mistakes at work he'd brushed off as "bad luck." For the first time, James couldn't hide from the numbers.

That led to Intentional Acceptance. He didn't wave the white flag or declare himself powerless. Instead, he acknowledged reality as it was, not as he wished it to be. He accepted that alcohol was running the show, and that if he didn't change, he'd lose more than just his health. He'd lose his family's trust, his professional credibility, and eventually himself. Acceptance wasn't surrender; it was clarity.

Then came Strategic Accountability, which he found to be the most challenging. He was the guy people leaned on, not the one who admitted weakness. But accountability wasn't about shame. It was about taking ownership. James established routines, set problematic guardrails around his evenings, and told a trusted friend what he was working on. That wasn't easy. He stumbled, more than once. There were nights he slipped, and mornings he wanted to quit. But instead of hiding, he owned it. He didn't blame stress, the job, or his family. He took responsibility, and in that responsibility, he found power.

By the time James reached Empowered Action, something shifted. He wasn't just talking about change; he was living it. He swapped out his after-work "happy hour" for an actual hour with his kids in the yard. He used his mornings for exercise instead of recovery. He rebuilt trust with his wife by showing up sober, present, and consistent. And the best part? He told me, "For the first time in years, I feel like I'm not surviving. I'm leading my life again."

That is Empowered Action. Not perfection, not never slipping, but taking full ownership of your life, getting up every time you fall down, and pushing forward with much better clarity and strength. Not only did James stop drinking, but he reclaimed himself.

Taking action only works when it's inspired, not forced. Inspired by your own deep understanding of why the status quo *is*, and why it needs to change, and supported by a commitment to using your own will to change it.

For years, I tried to muscle my way into sobriety through sheer will*power*. I'd wake up hungover, disgusted with myself, and declare that today was going to be different. I'd dump out bottles, throw away bottle openers, and make elaborate plans for how I was going to fill my evenings with productive activities instead of drinking. I'd attack the problem with the same aggressive determination I used for everything else in my life.

And it would work, for a few days, maybe a week or two. Then something would happen—a stressful day, a social situation, or just the accumulated exhaustion of white-knuckling through every evening—and I'd be right back where I started. Except now I had the additional burden of feeling like a failure on top of everything else.

The problem wasn't that I wasn't taking action. The problem was that I was taking *desperate* action instead of inspired, *empowered* action. I was acting from panic, shame, and self-hatred rather than from clarity, commitment, and self-respect. I was trying to run away from my current situation instead of walking toward a vision of the powerful man I wanted to become.

Desperate action is unsustainable because it's fueled by negative emotions that eventually burn out. Inspired action is sustainable because it's fueled by a positive vision that grows stronger over time when reinforced by even small successes and shifts. That's how we model Empowered Action.

If you've been stuck in the cycle of starting and stopping, promising and failing, getting motivated and losing steam, you're not lazy or broken. You're just trying to take action before you've done the foundational work that makes action effective. You're trying to build a house without laying a foundation first.

I see this pattern all the time with the executives, healthcare workers, and military personnel I work with. They're used to solving problems through immediate action. See a problem, attack the problem, solve the problem. It's served them well in their careers, so they apply the same approach to their drinking.

Alcoholism isn't a problem you can solve through force. It's a pattern you have to outgrow through understanding, acceptance, and strategic change. The action that works isn't frantic and desperate— it's calm and intentional.

Jeff, the IT Specialist I mentioned earlier, tried the aggressive approach for months before we started working together. "I treated my drinking like any regular problem," he told me. "Identify the issue, plan the intervention, execute with precision. But every time I 'quit drinking,' I felt like I was holding my breath. I knew I couldn't maintain that level of tension forever."

That's the difference between forced action and inspired action. Forced action feels like holding your breath. Inspired action feels like finally being able to breathe.

When Jeff started working with me, we didn't focus on what he was going to stop doing. We focused on who he was going to become. Not the person who drinks too much, but the person who doesn't need to drink. Not someone who's fighting against alcohol, but someone who's building toward clarity.

The action that emerged from that foundation was completely different. Instead of dumping out bottles in dramatic gestures of commitment, he redesigned his evening routine around activities that actually energized him. Instead of avoiding social situations where there would be alcohol, he started showing up as someone who simply didn't drink. No explanations needed, no internal conflict present.

Most importantly, instead of measuring success by how long he could go without drinking, he started measuring it by how present and authentic he felt in his daily life. The focus shifted from restriction to expansion, from managing symptoms to building solutions.

That's what Empowered Action looks like: It doesn't feel like fighting against your old life, it feels like building your new one.

This is exactly why you can't skip the first three steps and jump straight to action. Without *awareness*, you don't know what you're really dealing with. Without *acceptance*, you're still minimizing the problem or making excuses. Without *accountability*, you're still waiting for external circumstances to change before you fully commit. But when you've done that foundational work— when you see clearly what you're dealing with, accept the reality of your situation, and take complete ownership of the solution—taking *action* becomes natural rather than forced. It flows from clarity rather than desperation. It's sustainable rather than exhausting.

I often remind people: *Sobriety isn't just about removing the alcohol; it's about reclaiming the inner authority you gave away long before the first drink.* But you can't *reclaim* authority you haven't identified, accepted, and owned. And you can't effectively *use* authority without taking Empowered Action to direct it.

This isn't about willpower or discipline or forcing yourself to do things you don't want to do. This is about alignment: taking action that feels consistent with who you're becoming rather than action that feels like punishment for who you've been.

When I work with clients, we don't create action plans based on what they think they should do or what worked for someone else. We create action plans based on what feels authentic and sustainable for their specific situation, personality, and goals. Empowered Action has to feel like an expression of their values, not a violation of their preferences.

This is why the Battle Ready Framework *works*. It prepares you for the work ahead.

The cost of premature or misaligned action is enormous. Every time you take action that's not rooted in genuine commitment and clear understanding, you erode your self-trust a little bit more. Every failed attempt at forced sobriety makes the next attempt feel less possible. Every cycle of starting and stopping reinforces the belief that you can't really change.

But when action is aligned—when it flows from the solid foundation of awareness, acceptance, and accountability— it builds confidence instead of eroding it. Success becomes evidence of what's possible rather than a temporary reprieve from what's inevitable.

Dennis, the government worker I mentioned in the first chapter, put it this way: "The difference was that I wasn't trying to quit drinking, I was building a life I didn't need to escape from. The action felt like construction, not demolition."

That's the shift that changes everything. From trying to tear down old patterns to building new ones. From trying to avoid alcohol to creating conditions where alcohol becomes irrelevant. From fighting against your current identity to growing into your authentic one.

Empowered Action that flows from this foundation *doesn't* feel like work. It feels like coming home to yourself. Nor does it feel like a sacrifice. It feels like *an investment*. Instead of giving something up, it feels like *gaining everything back*.

This is crucial to understand: it isn't about doing more things. It's about doing the right things from the right place. It's about quality over quantity, alignment over effort, and sustainability over intensity. Most people try to solve their drinking problem by adding more rules, more restrictions, and more activities to fill the time they used to spend drinking. That's still operating from the old paradigm of force and control.

Empowered Action is different. *It's about becoming someone who doesn't want to drink, not someone who wants to drink but can't.* It's about building internal conditions that naturally lead to external behaviors, not trying to control external behaviors through internal force.

This is the action that creates lasting change: Action that's rooted in vision rather than desperation, alignment rather than force, growth rather than restriction feels like an expression of who you're becoming rather than a rejection of who you've been.

When you take action from this place, everything changes. Not just your drinking, but your confidence, your relationships, your sense of what's possible for your life. You stop being someone who's trying not to drink and become someone who simply doesn't need to. *Instead of being someone who's managing a problem, you become someone who's building a solution.*

Empowered Action alone isn't enough. Once you start taking aligned action and begin to see results, you need to build systems that support and sustain that momentum. You need to create an environment that makes success inevitable rather than dependent on constant willpower and discipline. That's where the real transformation happens: when you stop fighting against your environment and systems and start designing what naturally supports your new identity. Are you ready to build a life so compelling that alcohol becomes completely irrelevant?

If so, I'll be right beside you.

NEXT STEPS

You've made it this far. You've walked through the hard truths, you've seen the blind spots, and you've been given a framework to take your power back. But let me be honest with you: reading this book isn't the finish line, it's the starting point. Information alone doesn't change lives; *action does*.

So now you've got a decision to make. Here are your three options:

Option 1: Change Nothing

You can put this book down, slide it onto a shelf, and keep living exactly how you've been living. Stay in the same routines. Keep numbing out. Keep convincing yourself that "tomorrow" you'll figure it out.

I get it: this is the option I chose for years. It's tempting because it feels safe. Your comfort zone whispers, "Don't rock the boat.

Don't risk it. Just keep it together the way you always have." And I know firsthand how convincing that voice can be.

Yet here's the brutal truth: If you change nothing, nothing changes. The same mornings, the same guilt, the same fog, the same wasted potential. I wasted years thinking I could just wait it out. All the waiting ever did was cost me time I'll never get back.

Option 2: Do It Yourself

This is where most people land. You decide, "I don't need help. I can handle this on my own." And hey, it's a step up from doing nothing. I respect the drive behind that choice.

If you go this route, remember what you've learned here, especially about accountability. You'll need to build your own structure, track your own patterns, and be brutally honest when you slip. You'll need to create a plan rooted in clarity and commitment, not shame and willpower.

But let me give you some more straight talk: you've probably tried this before. I know I did. I told myself I could figure it out, that I was disciplined enough to manage it. And sometimes, it even worked… for a little while. Then the old patterns came back, stronger than before.

Can you make progress alone? Sure. But it's slower, harder, and lonelier than it has to be. And if you try this path, put a hard deadline on it. If your life hasn't drastically improved in a month or two, don't lie to yourself. Don't drag it out. Be willing to pivot.

Option 3: Talk to Me

Notice I didn't say "hire me." I said: *Talk* to me. That's it. One conversation. No pressure, no contracts. Just two people talking—one who's been where you are, and one who knows there's a way out.

For me, there was no conversation, no mentor, no guide. I wish someone had shown up with the right words, but they didn't. I did it the hard way, through trial, error, and sheer refusal to stay stuck. If you're reading this, I hope that you don't waste the time I did. I can't walk the path for you, but I can walk the path with you, and hand you the map I never had.

I've had countless clients tell me the same thing: "If I hadn't made that call, I'd still be stuck." Sometimes it's not about taking a giant leap; it's about taking the first step. So instead of doing nothing… or grinding through another lonely round of trying to figure it out yourself … reach out. Let's talk. At the very least, I can walk you through the results of my No Regrets Quiz and help you understand where you are and what options you really have.

You *don't* have to walk this road alone. You don't have to *stay stuck* in the same cycle. You don't have to waste *one more day*.

Reach out to me at tim@7secretpillarsofsobriety.com or visit my website at **7secretpillarsofsobriety.com** to learn more about how I work. Let this be the start of your next chapter. Because the moment you decide to *act*—not someday, not tomorrow, but *now*—that's the moment your real life begins.

THE OTHER SIDE OF HIGH-FUNCTIONING HELL

People always ask me how I knew I was done with alcohol, how I went from a high-functioning alcoholic to what I like to call a "retired alcoholic." The fact is, there wasn't a lightning bolt moment. No angels, no sudden freedom.

It was more like waking up from a decades-long dream, realizing I'd been stuck at 17. The kid who discovered alcohol could make pain vanish.

As I rose in the military, made life-or-death decisions, and gained respect, part of me remained frozen as that insecure teenager. Alcohol was my medicine for never feeling enough.

When the suffering lifted–not so much the drinking itself, but the shame, guilt, and lies I told myself- I didn't feel powerful. But I felt clear. As if someone had finally flipped on the lights in a room I'd been stumbling through for years in the dark.

That clarity shifted everything. Not overnight but gradually.

I wanted to be present, not just physically there, but emotionally available.

I wanted to help other high-functioning men who appeared strong in the boardroom or briefing room but were quietly struggling inside. I wanted to show them what I wish someone had told me: You're not broken. You've just been trained wrong.

That insight became the foundation of my work. I serve high-functioning alcoholics, men who have too much to lose to take a chance at traditional group programs or public recovery. These are not people in barroom brawls or Hollywood stories of rehab. They are surgeons, lawyers, commanders, leaders, still achieving on paper while alcohol eats them alive.

This is what I believe: These men do not need to be broken down further. They don't need shame, labels, or endless meetings. They don't need to surrender their power. They need to redirect it. They need strategies, tools, and accountability tailored to their unique lives, careers, and goals.

Some hate when I use the word "cure." The recovery business insists that alcoholism is a chronic disease to be managed, not solved. However, evidence from my life, as well as from the lives of my clients, suggests otherwise. You can retrain your brain, change your habits, and redefine your identity. Peace doesn't come from decades of white knuckling it through meetings. It's achieved by doing the deeper work that traditional programs often overlook.

But here's the catch: It only works when everything is done in the correct order. Awareness without acceptance is useless. Acceptance without accountability is hollow. Accountability without action is stuck. And action without a base is futile. Most people want to skip steps, but skipping steps leads to failure sooner.

The clients I assist are those who are ready to do the work. Not because they're broken, but because they're done lying to themselves. They value truth more than comfort, and prioritize change over excuses, as well as freedom over management. You do not have to hit rock bottom. You're not powerless. You're not doomed to recovery meetings for the rest of your natural life. It's the opposite; high-functioning alcoholics are extremely powerful. Their power is misdirected. When it is redirected, they want to live their lives as people who want to drink and can't. They live and no longer want it.

That's what I want for you. Not endless management, but freedom. Not sobriety that feels deprived, but sobriety that feels like coming home.

The Battle Ready Framework is not about sacrificing anything. It's about reclaiming your life. It's about taking back the authority over your life that you gave away long before your first drink.

So, the question isn't whether you can change. You can. The question is whether you are ready to do the work that change demands.

ABOUT THE AUTHOR

Raised in chaos, forged in the military, and tested by addiction, Tim Murphy's life is proof that resilience is possible. Once a suicidal teenage alcoholic, he went on to serve 30 years in the U.S. Air Force before finally confronting the enemy within.

Now sober and thriving, Tim shares his hard-earned lessons to guide others out of survival mode and into freedom.

ACKNOWLEDGMENTS

To my grandmother, Margie Murphy, I know you're smiling down on me. You stepped in to raise my brothers and me at a time when you should have been enjoying your retirement. Your strength and sacrifice shaped who I am today, and I will carry that gratitude for the rest of my life.

To my kids, Kimberly, Ellis, and Kyle, thank you for your unconditional love and for giving me the greatest reason to stay the course. You inspire me every day to keep becoming the man and father you deserve.

To my publishing team, led by Lin Eleoff at AFGO Press. Thank you for your wisdom, your patience, and your commitment to helping me bring this message into the world.

To my friends and supporters, you stood by me when the path wasn't clear, and your belief helped me keep moving forward.

And finally, to the readers holding this book. You are why I wrote it. This journey isn't easy, but you don't have to walk it alone. If my story gives you even one spark of hope, then every word here was worth writing.

BEFORE YOU GO...

The No Regrets Quiz

The **No Regrets Quiz** was created to show you whether the alcohol is still in balance in your life, or if you may have more of a problem than you have been willing to admit up to this point. It's designed to highlight the compromises you may be making for the alcohol that, if you're like me, you may come to regret down the line. It's short and insightful and it's free. You'll find it at **7secretpillarsofsobriety.com**.

Want the Cheat Sheet?

Would you like a cheat sheet of the Battle Ready Framework to help remind you of the four steps you'll need to take to go from high-functioning hell to empowered living? Send an email to tim@7pillarsofsobriety.com and put SEND ME THE CHEAT SHEET in the subject line.

7 Secret Pillars of Sobriety

The Battle Ready Framework is just the beginning. It lays the foundation for my signature coaching program, **7 Secret Pillars of Sobriety**. A proven system that takes people from struggling in silence to living with strength, clarity, and lasting sobriety. This program is where the real transformation occurs, providing you with the tools, structure, and support to build a sober life that you actually enjoy.

To learn more or to join the program, visit:

7secretpillarsofsobriety.com

Thank you for your interest in

ALCOHOLICS ARE LIARS

A Field Manual for High-Functioning
(Over)Drinkers

By Tim Murphy

AP

Published by AFGO Press

AFGO Press is a division of AFGO Media
and Publishing, whose mission is to support
women in building their own businesses.

**For more information, go to
AFGOmedia.com**

www.ingramcontent.com/pod-product-compliance
Lightning Source LLC
Chambersburg PA
CBHW021139020426
42331CB00005B/839